Asperger Syndrome,
the Universe and Everything

of related interest

Freaks, Geeks and Asperger Syndrome
A User Guide to Adolescence
Luke Jackson
ISBN 1 84310 098 3

**Finding Out About Asperger's Syndrome,
High Functioning Autism and PDD**
Gunilla Gerland
ISBN 1 85302 840 1

Parents' Education as Autism Therapists
Applied Behaviour Analysis in Context
Edited by Mickey Keenan, Ken P. Kerr and Karola Dillenburger
ISBN 1 85302 778 2

The Self-Help Guide for Special Kids and their Parents
Joan Matthews and James Williams
ISBN 1 85302 914 9

Asperger's Syndrome
A Guide for Parents and Professionals
Tony Attwood
ISBN 1 85302 749 9

Kenneth passes GCSE Maths
– six years ahead of time

Asperger Syndrome, the Universe and Everything

Kenneth Hall

Forewords by Ken P. Kerr and Gill Rowley

Jessica Kingsley Publishers
London and New York

The photograph of Kenneth's class at the Steiner School is reproduced with the school's kind permission.

First published in the United Kingdom in 2001 by
Jessica Kingsley Publishers Ltd,
116 Pentonville Road,
London N1 9JB,
England
and
29 West 35th Street, 10th fl.
New York, NY 10001–2299, USA

www.jkp.com

Copyright © 2001 Kenneth Hall

Second impression 2001
Third imperssion 2002
Fourth impression 2003

Library of Congress Cataloging in Publication Data
A CIP catalog record for this book is available from the Library of Congress

British Library Cataloguing in Publication Data
A CIP catalogue record for this book is available from the British Library

ISBN 1 85302 930 0

Printed and Bound in Great Britain by
Athenaeum Press, Gateshead, Tyne and Wear

Contents

Foreword

To say that I am delighted with this book, which adds to our understanding of Asperger's Syndrome (AS), is an understatement. As a behaviour analyst, I have been consistently impressed by the creativity shown by both Kenneth Hall and his mum, Brenda. Before I continue let me explain how I first met Kenneth and Brenda. I met Brenda at a meeting of the Parent's Education as Autism Therapists (PEAT) group, which allows parents to become familiar with and skilled in Applied Behaviour Analysis (ABA). Using ABA as a vehicle, Brenda and Kenneth have devised a dynamic educational programme over the last few years, which has helped Kenneth become motivated to engage in many different areas of behaviour.

In terms of motivation and learning, behaviour analysts are taught the phrase 'the learner knows best' and throughout my professional life I have tried to honour this. It is a remarkable achievement by Kenneth that he, as the learner, has created this opportunity to share his views of the world. It is a healthy thing for people of any age to learn to take responsibility for their own behaviour. For Kenneth, this responsibility has come through participation as a partner in an individualised system of education. It is a tribute to the efficacy of ABA, its positive nature, and the input from various educational professionals that Kenneth holds his programme in such high regard.

Another indication of the responsibility and maturity that Kenneth exhibits is the fact that he felt it his mission to write this book to help others understand AS. Parents, family members, and professionals will find that Kenneth's story offers a fascinating insight into the life of an individual with AS. From a point where Kenneth did not understand his difference, to a point where he accepts the differences and is proud of who he is, this book is a must for those studying AS.

I am proud to have been part of a team of educationalists who have supported Kenneth and Brenda in their work. In Kenneth's words: 'Once you've started the search for wisdom, you can't stop.' Our search for wisdom involves recognition of the needs, desires, and differences of children like Kenneth. We, as parents and professionals, should strive to be partners in education with children in continuing this search for wisdom. This book shows Kenneth to be a willing learner and a skilled teacher when it comes to AS. It represents another step along the road of discovery for parents, children, and professionals alike.

Ken P. Kerr D.Phil, C. Psychol
Director of Training, PEAT

Foreword

I can think of only one completely true short definition of gifted and talented children – that they are all different and that, in most cases, they possess highly individual and complex personalities. It is also true that if they do not find a compatible learning environment, most such children will fail to realize their potential and suffer from some degree of under-achievement and frustration. For the intellectually gifted child with a learning difficulty this is doubly the case.

We talk of teachers teaching 'a class' rather than a group of many very different children, often of mixed ability, varied social and ethnic backgrounds and with a proportion of 'special' or 'additional' needs. The gifted child with Asperger Syndrome, ADHD, dyslexia, dyspraxia, sensory impairment, brain damage or physical handicap can often not receive much individual direction at all.

The National Association for Gifted Children has campaigned for a fairer distribution of classroom resources and an equally challenging education for all children for over thirty years. The Association has been aware of the incidence of high ability combined with a specific learning disorder and is now looking further into this with the help of DfEE funding.

Problems abound. It is therefore all the more refreshing to read 10-year-old Kenneth's positive and individual outlook on his situation. His educational needs are clearly being met by his family and supportive LEA – the local Education Board in Northern Ireland – and there is clear evidence that after a faltering start, Kenneth will leap on with enthusiasm to overcome his difficulties and lead an intellectually and emotionally fulfilling life.

NAGC would wish that all such children have this chance and that Kenneth's book will go some way to raising awareness of the problems and possibilities of highly gifted children with a known learning difficulty.

Gill Rowley
Chairman
National Association for Gifted Children
October 2000

Chapter One

Who Am I?

A few things about me

Hello. I'm Kenneth Hall and I'm ten years old. I am a fair-haired, blue-eyed boy. I like to keep my hair at Number Four length. I am thinnish and smallish and I like to wear smart, comfortable clothes. People tell me that I've a nice smile and I like to think of myself as friendly, kind and thoughtful.

I admire kindness, patience and helpfulness in people and I like a good sense of humour.

I am also very determined which is a good thing about me. People who are easily led never get anywhere.

I am very interested in words and I make a lot of jokes. For instance, recently when I heard my mum saying:

'That's a turn up for the books.'

I said:

'And a potato too if they really want it!'

Mum didn't understand at first. Sometimes people don't understand my sense of humour.

Me and Asperger Syndrome

When I was eight I found out about my Asperger Syndrome or AS and since then my life has changed completely. Before that life was very hard for me. I was always depressed. Life was depressing.

I always knew I was different and that I wasn't quite like other children. It's hard to say exactly how I knew. I detected some differences and I felt that things were not the same for me as for other children. Other children seemed to behave differently, play differently and talk differently, but I didn't know why. At that time, although I felt different I felt normal about being different. I thought I was the normal one and that it was the other people who were different, not me. Which is a perfectly feasible way of thinking.

When I heard that I had AS I was very pleased because I had been wondering why everyone else seemed to be acting strangely. So I felt a bit relieved.

My life has completely changed now and I am much happier. Things are much better and I understand myself better than I used to. Children with AS can do very well if they have a positive attitude, but they also need a lot of positive things around them and this is mostly up to the adults.

People help me and treat me better now. For example my Mum. I can't explain how she helps me. I just know that she does somehow. Lots of other people help me too – like Kate Doherty and Ken Kerr and Leo and Julie May. And the Education Board. (For any people who don't know, the Education Board is a government department which has people who help kids.) Julie Connell for example. She helped by getting me the laptop and she is the one got me started off on writing this book.

Another thing which has helped me a lot is Applied Behavioural Analysis, or ABA. This works by breaking goals down into small steps with rewards like tokens and prizes for each one. It is really good fun.

I like being different. I prefer having AS to being normal. I don't have the foggiest idea exactly what it

is I like about AS. I think that people with AS see things differently. I also think they see them more clearly.

When I first heard I had AS I was sure God must have had a reason for making me different. I am still convinced about this. I also wondered what was God's special mission for me. I was quite determined to find out and I still am. Perhaps writing this book is part of it but I don't know.

About my life

Where I live

I live in a place called Northern Ireland. Our house is about five miles from Belfast and it is near the sea. Where we live is quite high up on a hill. There is less risk of floods on a hill, which is one good thing.

Northern Ireland is a very peace-loving place, which often has no peace. Most people in all parts of Ireland want peace but there has always been a lot of fighting over who rules us. Some people think we should rule ourselves. Some people think the Republic of Ireland should rule us, and some people think it should be Britain. So you can see the problem. I would love there to be perfect peace. It is silly for different religions to fight each other.

We live in a really nice house now. Once I did a cool house plan which shows every room and the exact position of all the furniture and you can see how to get from room to room. Willie helped me do this on the computer at his office. He is an architect and he is Julie May's husband.

When I was very small we lived in a house with a tiny kitchen. It was a very short distance from one side to the other. I bet that I could easily jump it now in one long jump. I remember it a bit but I love this house. It feels just like home, especially my room. This one is where we found out about my AS so I like it best.

My memories so far

BEFORE I WAS BORN

I remember my Mum before either of us was born and when I remember her it is at any age. I remember being very cosy before I was born. I think God removes most of the memories about our non-physical life when we come here because it is hard to remember more than about ten seconds of it. I can remember about seven seconds which is more than most probably.

I remember being with Mum and we were both children. We were walking beside each other on a grassy open place and no-one else was about. I was very relaxed and happy. In this world the closest I ever get to this feeling is if I am lying all cosy in my sleeping bag with Sandy, my cat, near me. Then I feel glad to be in this world and not homesick.

Granpa holding me when I was a baby

WHEN I WAS A BABY

I don't remember much about being a baby, except the time I was trying to climb up a chest of drawers and then I fell. My mind just blanks off at that point – I think it was very traumatic for me. It makes me very nervous even trying to remember it now. All I can remember is pain and shock, seeing some red stuff and crying.

That is when I got the scar on my forehead. It is not too noticeable now unless I have a summer tan. Harry Potter has a scar on his forehead too. Mine might be like Harry Potter's, but mine is like true lightning not the jagged lightning you see in pictures.

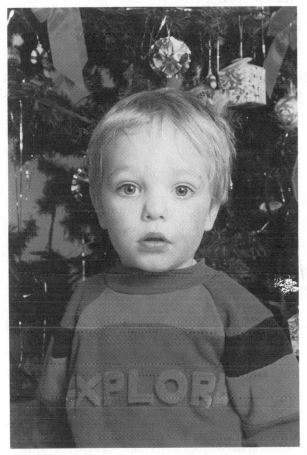

Me as a toddler standing in front of the Christmas tree

MERRYGOROUND PLAYGROUP

When I was three I started going to a playgroup called MerryGoRound which I can only remember a bit. I got used to it so I was miserable when I had to leave there to start school. I also remember Barbara my childminder and getting rides in the furniture lorry.

PRIMARY SCHOOL

The start of my primary school was very traumatic for me, because it was so new. I hated nearly everything about it. Having to sit still. The other children. The handwriting. The work. It was very easy and very boring. I hated the noise of school but I am not sure exactly what part of it I hated. Playing was boring. In the playground I always tried to find a quiet corner. In the classroom I mostly tried to find a quiet corner and do nothing at all. I can't say anything at all about what my behaviour was like because I can't remember.

There were a lot of problems and I had difficulties trying to cope. I thought I would get used to it but I didn't. I never quite adjusted to it and I was even sent to the headmaster. This got me very annoyed because I was definitely blamed wrongly.

One of the things that caused trouble was when I refused to handwrite. This caused problems till I was

nine. Then Mum used ABA to get me started on joined-up handwriting. After that Julie May took over. I still hate handwriting. It is usually boring and pointless, but then this is true for a lot of things adults try to get children to do.

RUDOLF STEINER SCHOOL

When I was seven Mum moved me to a different school. This was because of all the problems at the primary school. The new school was called the Rudolf Steiner School. For the first year I went into the kindergarten. I was the very oldest child in the whole kindergarten and in the kindergarten the children were allowed to play instead of having lessons.

That school was easier for me but I still had difficulties. The teachers were nicer. They listened to you instead of giving off. I had a better time there but it was still very hard.

When I was eight I went into Class One. I had a very kind teacher called Jacinta. I still like to see her

Jacinta, my teacher, and the class at the Steiner School. I am second from the right in the row which is sitting on the chairs.
This photograph is reproduced with the kind permission of the Steiner School.

sometimes when I go to visit the school or else she comes to visit me. One thing that spoiled it was the groups of children. I have a lot of trouble when there are about four or more other children around. I don't know what causes this problem.

One difficulty was I couldn't interact properly with a group. It can be hard to be a kid who does not want to be part of any of the groups. I did not like to do my work at school. It was a bit better when Jacinta let me take it home to do. I liked painting but not with the other children around.

The best bit at the Steiner School was when I started getting out of class to see Joan once a week. She taught me on my own in her room and I loved that. Another thing I liked at the Steiner School was gardening.

At both schools I definitely hated handwriting. In fact I still do. I didn't really do much writing at all till I started it at home using ABA. Since then I've developed my handwriting very well. Here is a sample of my writing now.

My handwriting

HOME SCHOOLING

When I stopped going to school over a year ago I started being tutored at home instead. I have ten hours' tutoring a week now. Julie May is my main tutor. One of my first two tutors has now left. Her name was Dawn, and so when she was late I used to say she should come at the crack of herself.

For a while I was only tutored by Julie May, but then Lorna started working on Fridays. All my tutors are very nice and kind.

The best thing about tutoring is that you can work at your own pace and there are no distractions like other children. Usually I don't want to do any handwriting. When I don't want to write, they try to persuade me by saying that I won't be allowed something else fun later. Fun things in tutoring are things like science experiments. I usually don't see the point in writing. I can think or talk much quicker. At least ten times quicker.

Using a laptop is better fun than handwriting. I use mine a lot. I can do a bit of touch typing but I am still faster when I look at the keys.

DREAMS / NIGHTMARES

Sometimes I used to have a nightmare where I was blown away by a strong wind. I was looking for my Dad and had a terrible fear I'd not be able to find

him. Then I found my
friend who was driving a car
even though he was very
young. My friend took me
in his car and he helped me
find my Dad in the end. The
dream left me with a weird
feeling. But God doesn't let nightmares get beyond
a certain stage of scariness.

When we go to sleep sometimes we go to
different places. For example we can go into a third
heaven. This is where music comes from. One of the
saints managed to get into the third heaven. I have
no idea how I know this or where this information
came from.

People in my life

The most important people in my life are my close
family including Sandy, my cat. I would not like to
leave them for any more than about two minutes.

My stepdad Chris is gifted in patience and he is
always calm. In children's stories the step-relations
are always wicked but this is completely untrue in
real life. Chris writes computer software for lots of
companies and helps them sort out their problems. I
used his software to set up a company called Wallace

& Gromit & Co. and printed out invoices for the inventions.

This is Chris and me on Free Spirit

My sister Christine is gifted in kindness and knowing the right thing to do. Gerard is her boyfriend and they are usually together. I like him a lot. He is one of those people you just like. Christine is twenty and she loves fashion. She is always buying new clothes and shoes which are fashionable. Ladies often wear high heeled shoes to be in the fashion. This is really silly because it cramps up their toes and makes it hard for them to walk or run. I do not know why ladies follow fashion so much. This is something I can't really explain.

Me, Christine and Gerard in our kitchen. This was the day after Christine's twentieth birthday.

Mum says Christine loves spending money. I think if she got married it would be better because then she could spend the money on useful things like paying bills. I prefer to  save my pocket money. Once I bought two Furbies with my own money and I regretted it. I got fed up with them after about six hours because they were a nuisance. Some of the best things I ever bought were a steering wheel for my PlayStation and a GameBoy.

Gerard is a footballer. He is a semi-professional. Christine might marry Gerard. This would mean I would have a brother-in-law. I don't know why it is called brother-in-law even if they are married in a church. Why is it not brother-in-religion? If he became my brother-in-law, it would not be quite as good as a blood brother, but it would still be good.

Dad looking straight at the camera

My Dad is great fun, but sometimes he can get a bit cross. One thing I will never do is start smoking.

Trying to stop smoking is what can make him a bit grumpy. He has a very kind heart. I would give him nine out of ten. My Mum would also get nine out of ten, but that's pretty good. No-one (except God) could get ten out of ten.

I go to my Dad's house quite a lot and he plays with me. Once I got a new cap and I wore it to my Dad's house. My Dad said:

'That's a super cap. I wish I had a cap like that.'

I bought my Dad a cap the exact same for Father's Day. When I gave him his new cap, he was delighted and pleased. This just goes to show that you get your wish granted whether you keep it secret or not, as long as you're kind.

I have two grannies and no grandpas. Both my grannies live in Northern Ireland. They are both very kind and one has white hair. The other one is Mum's mum and she spoils me a lot with Twix bars and jellybeans. She is very kind but she can't hear or walk very well.

I have also got a Nanna Margaret who is Chris's aunt. She gave me raspberry canes for Christmas one year. This was one of my favourite Christmas presents because it was a growing and a sharing present. We got big crops even from the first season. One day when Mum said that the raspberries were out early, and I said: 'Yes, it's only nine AM!'

This is Granny standing in our kitchen

We make jam to give to friends which is delicious – far, far nicer than any jam that you get at the shops.

The other people I see a lot are my tutors. Tutoring is better than school. Julie May comes on Mondays, Tuesdays and Wednesdays and Lorna comes on Fridays which means I get every Thursday off. This is a lot better than most kids get.

My favourite things

My favourite creature in the world: Sandy

Sandy, my cat is a very important member of my family. He is the cutest wee cat in the world. He is about thirteen months old, and he is bigger than

Bella and Jess who are fully grown cats. This is because he stuffs himself non-stop. He is the exact opposite of me in that way. But in other ways we are just the same. For example we are both cat lovers.

Sandy is the cutest wee cat in the world. (I say this all the time.) I didn't go with Mum when she got him. It was a surprise. When I came in she said there was a surprise for me. I didn't know if it would be a good surprise or a bad surprise.

Me holding Sandy. Sandy looks adorable of course.

I nearly sat down on the settee on top of him, except I heard this purring. We made friends immediately. I spoil him a lot. How I spoil him is with too much food, too much attention and letting him get away with blue murder and red and black and yellow murder as well!

When I got him Mum and I spent a long time training him and now he comes to his name which is very unusual for a cat. We used ABA which is something I am very good at now. Sandy likes his food a lot which is  the exact opposite of me so we used Kitbits and strokes for the training. Kitbits are special cat food treats. First Mum called him and rewarded him with Kitbits and strokes, then I did the same, over and over.

My favourite places to be: Quiet places

I like quiet places best, such as my room, and I like to spend a lot of time playing or reading on my own. I like to spend a lot of time at home in my house. Sometimes I don't like to go out much. I like my room a lot. This is because it makes me feel brilliant, cosy and happy. The best thing about my room is that it is homely – roomly if you want to be very accurate.

I like to sleep in a sleeping bag at night, which I do almost all the time. Even during the day I like to be in my sleeping bag as much as possible I love it so much. My sleeping bag feels brilliant; it is so cosy. The fabric of it is just perfect.

I have a super bed, which is a mattress on the floor and my sleeping bag. There are curtains all the way round the bed like a den. It's really cosy inside and I

This is Mum and me. We were both having a great time.

love being cosy! So I spend a lot of time in my room and in my sleeping bag, on my own with no-one disturbing me. This is my absolute favourite thing to do.

My favourite days are what I call jammie days. On jammie days I am allowed to stay in my jammies all day and do not have to do anything. I do not even have to come out of my room if I don't want to. Usually I hate having to do the things that adults want me to do because they are pointless and boring. Jammie days are better than anything because they seem like the only days when I can really relax. On jammie days I stay on my own in my sleeping bag, in my room and read a lot which is what I love to do best in the world.

The sort of thing I absolutely hate is if Mum has promised me a jammie day and then she arranges to do something else instead. I hate it because it spoils the jammie day completely; and also because it means that a promise has been broken.

Once Mum tried to spoil a jammie day so we could go and visit Anne Marie. I was extremely angry because she had not consulted me at all about it. I refused to go because this was a promise broken. I had been looking forward to my jammie day all week. Jammie days are very important to me.

Holidays

For holidays we go to the caravan at Portstewart. We stay at a very quiet caravan park. It is so quiet you would hardly know it was there. You could easily drive past the entrance and not see it. There are not usually too many people about. When I am at the caravan I spend a lot of time being very cosy in my sleeping bag on my bunk. I love this because being cosy is one of my favourite things to be, and I have lots of books at the caravan.

There is a really clean beach and sand dunes, which you can explore. I love the sand and the ocean. Sometimes I feel as if I was born for the sea. I love everything to do with the sea – the sound, the sight and the atmosphere. I like it best when it is quiet because it makes me feel peaceful. The perfect time to be by the sea is at sunset especially if there are hardly any people about.

Sometimes we walk all the way to the Barmouth and back. This is a five mile walk along the sand. The sand is a beautiful colour. Like my pet cat, Sandy. He is a sort of in between sand and snow colour. If you put Sandy on top of the sand at

Portstewart you would hardly even know he was there.

Sometimes we go along by the Number Ten route. We have found a quiet beach there that hardly anyone knows about. The Number Ten route takes a lot longer because you have to go right round the sand dunes. But it is good fun with all the climbing.

My favourite things to do

My absolute favourite thing to do is to spend a lot of time in my room with Sandy and my sleeping bag and no-one disturbing me. Here are some of the things I might do on my own:

READING

I spend a lot of time reading because it is one of my favourite things to do. I've read hundreds of books in my life and if books were food I would be very fat. I wasn't ever taught how to read. I just discovered how when I was very young and I have enjoyed it ever since. I have over four hundred books which I keep in alphabetical order by author.

Some people say AS kids prefer to read factual books. This is definitely untrue. I would reckon about 97 per cent prefer fiction. I like adventure stories best. I would love to be a character out of an adventure in one of my books. Sometimes I like to read the same book over and over many times. I have read some of my very favourite books approximately 50–55 times.

My favourite author used to be Enid Blyton. I have read stacks and stacks of her books. My new favourite author is J.K. Rowling, author of the Harry Potter books. She has beaten Roald Dahl and C.S. Lewis and she has knocked Enid Blyton off the pedestal completely.

When I started to read the Harry Potter books I could not even put them down or stop thinking about them and I keep on reading them over again. I couldn't wait for the fourth one to be published. I had my name on the waiting list for months and I was one of the very first in the UK to get it. The postman brought it at 7.30am and I was so excited I could hardly put it down that day. It was brilliant! I had the whole book, which was 636 pages, read by that same afternoon.

I keep on rereading the Harry Potter books and I can't wait for numbers five, six and seven.

PLAYING

I like playing on my own best but sometimes I enjoy playing with one or two other children or with an adult. I usually find adults easiest to get on with. Sometimes I make up good games with lots of rules. I like Table Top Football and I beat Mum hands down every time. Sometimes I play this with Sandy, my cat.

I also enjoy climbing – big time! In our garden we have a beautiful oak tree which I like to climb. It is a giant oak. That is different from an ordinary oak. The 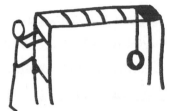 leaves are a lot bigger. In the garden we have scramble netting to climb and I also enjoy climbing round the furniture in the house which I do a lot.

The games I like playing best are computer games. I love computers games. In fact I love any-thing to do with computers. I like learning and playing on them. I especially like playing on my PlayStation. I got this at Christmas. Santa brought it to my Dad's house. That's one good thing about having two houses. Santa comes to both of them.

My favourite PlayStation game is 'Fifa Road to the World Cup '98'. I also like 'Lego Racer'. My Dad is very good at 'Formula 1'97', but I'm not. I watch the Grand Prix on TV with my dad sometimes. I wanted Eddie Irvine to win because he is from Conlig. This is where my cat came from. We got him from an animal sanctuary in Conlig called Assisi. He was in a rabbit hutch when we got him. The girl who first found him called him Sandy so we called him Sandy too. Her mum wouldn't let her keep him. He was wild before he was found.

Sometimes I like to play Wallace and Gromit. I am Gromit and Chris, my stepdad, is Wallace. He says I make a nice wee dog. I am very good at being Gromit. I help Wallace with lots of inventions and adventures. I even print out invoices and statements from the company, which I made up on my laptop. This is called Wallace & Gromit & Co.

COMPUTERS

I love working on computers and I use a laptop which I really enjoy. I got this from the Education Board. This is one of the few government departments which actually take kids seriously. My stepdad works with computers. He is a software writer and a real expert on computers. For Christmas he got me a modem, so now I can get onto the Internet. I have to ask permission to go on line because it costs money and engages the phone.

For my GCSE Maths coursework I used the computer quite a lot. I know quite a lot about computers, definitely more than either of my tutors.

Chapter Two

What Is Different About Me

It is hard for me to know for sure what is different about me because I just feel normal to myself. I think there are some differences about how I feel and learn things. Some things are easier and some are harder. I always try to work very hard at the things that are difficult for me. This is a very important thing to do.

My difficulties

Crowds

One thing I don't like is crowds. For example, I just hated the classroom. The noise annoyed me. At the time the sound of the children's chatter was like dynamite going off in my ears.

Concentrating

I find it impossible to concentrate on more than one thing at a time. And sometimes I find it hard to stop and move onto the next task. I don't like being asked something when I am already concentrating on something else. Sometimes I find it hard to start concentrating or remembering what I have been asked to do. Like most nights, when Mum asks me to get on my jammies I have to come and ask her ten minutes later what I am supposed to be doing!

Being patient and understanding others

Sometimes I find it difficult to be patient and small things might still upset me like someone leaving a drawer open. I try to understand how other people feel but sometimes I find it extremely difficult to know.

Attention

Usually I find it hard not to get attention. Sometimes I like to talk and be listened to a lot and I get really upset when I am ignored. I hate it when Mum starts to talk on the phone. Then she might chat on and on and on for ages. Or if I am out with my Mum and she meets a friend. Sometimes the person talks to me too or asks me questions, but I usually just ignore them. The reason I do this is because it is so boring. It makes me act very restless so I complain loudly and try to pull Mum away.

Other times I can't stand to have any attention at all and I need to be ignored and left in peace. When I feel like this I usually tell people to go away. It is cosy then to be in my room, curled up in my sleeping bag. I love my sleeping bag. I love it when Mum lets me stay in my sleeping bag in the kitchen or the hall. Or during the tutoring when Julie May lets me have it at break time.

Being part of a group

This is another thing which is extremely difficult for me. In groups I behave differently. I can't concentrate or be friendly at all. I get distracted easily.

The first time I meet someone I usually put them into one of two categories, friend or not, and then I don't like to change my mind about my decision.

I have a lot of trouble when there are about four or more other children around. I don't know what causes this problem but I think it is something to do with AS.

It is easiest to be with one other child at a time. This can make it difficult to have friends. But any friends that I make are very good friends and I would do my best to never let them down.

Staying still instead of twirling and leaping

I often find it hard to stay still and I have a lot of energy. I do stunts in the hall which I am quite good at. Quite often I don't stop jumping and twirling around and pummelling my cuddly toys, especially Leo.

I also love leaping around the furniture. I like to do this approximately every half hour, or even every fifteen minutes if I can manage it. I also enjoy making noises like 'Zzzhhh Zzzhhh' quite a lot. I like doing that. Sometimes I get dizzy which can be a nice feeling. Another thing I love is running along the side of the ocean and throwing stones into the water, or playing with the sand.

I love rough and tumble play and climbing on Chris's shoulders. It is a bit strange but I also love being squashed tight. Once we went to see a lady who told us a lot about the importance of relaxation. Then we got a Peanut Roll. Its proper name is a Physiotherapy Roll but we call it a Peanut Roll because it looks like an huge peanut. It is good fun. You can use it for squashing games or else you can just lie under it and have someone roll it right over you and squash you. This is very relaxing for me.

Making decisions and changes

Sometimes I find it very difficult making decisions. Then I might toss a coin – heads one choice; tails the other. Sometimes the coin gives me the wrong answer and I say 'best of three' or 'best of five'. It's funny how sometimes I don't really know what decision I want till after the coin has been tossed.

I prefer it when some things don't change too much. Lunch works best when it is the exact same each day. When I take grated cheese for lunch each day then I know where I stand. I like it to be with the proper grater – my own grater–, that is because it is horrible when it is grated too coarsely. I just can't take it. There is a perfect texture for cheese.

I am not at all keen on changes of plan. Especially if it is something like Mum promising me a jammie day and then trying to get me to do something else. Or someone coming to visit when I wasn't expecting them.

How I feel things

Senses

Senses help people feel and learn about things. Some people think there are only five senses but there are more than five. For example there is intuition.

I know a lot of things with my mind or spirit alone, not my body. Another one is the heavenly sense. This one is the most important. It tells us about God, but some people throw it away. God is like the stars, always there even if we don't see Him. He gives people special tasks and missions. I think my special mission might be to do with helping other kids with AS.

Pain

I think AS people sometimes feel things differently. They might be very sensitive. For me, one weird thing is I seem to be immune to certain pains. Like recently I was sick during the night without knowing it till the morning. Other times I feel things very intensely.

Noise

I like peaceful noises best. Like birds singing. Noises I absolutely hate are the hoover and the liquidiser, and also the sound of a lot of chatter.

I always get right out of the way when the hoover is going. I think the reason I panic with the hoover started back when I was small and I was worried that Mum was going to hoover up something important, like some of my toys. Then that panicky feeling spread to the liquidiser noise as well.

My hair

I am very sensitive about my hair. I really hate it touching my forehead. One thing I used to do a lot was to shake my head over and over. This was really because of the annoying hair problem. I don't have that problem any more now because of keeping my hair very short.

When I was small it annoyed me so much I used to rub my forehead hard with my jumper a lot. This made it sore and it came up in a bump. The grazed bit made me want to rub it even more so it got worse and worse.

These days I keep my hair very short. My Mum cuts it now at Number Four length. She got a home hair cutting set. This is excellent because it even saves money.

I used to go to the barber but in the end I just couldn't put up with him any more at all. I think he deliberately drove the scissors into me. I bet I could report him for cruelty. He literally injured me he was so rough and then he gave me a lolly at the end (I think this was a bribe but it did not work).

Taste and food

Another unusual thing about me is that I definitely can't take most foods. Eating is one of my biggest difficulties. I can't explain why I have this difficulty, but for me this is the worst thing about AS.

The thing I absolutely hate most is trying anything new. There are hardly any foods I eat at all. I especially hate any food with bits in it, or things mixed together with each other, like cheese mixed with bread in a cheese sandwich, or mixed colours of foods. Sometimes I can eat a bit better if I am left on my own.

One thing I quite like is grated Red Leicester cheese in a bowl. I take that for lunch every day now. Mum usually lets me grate it myself. We have three sizes of grater, including one size which is just perfect. This grates it very finely the way I like.

I don't like to eat any food which is the wrong texture. Pringles are the perfect texture, but the Pringles Right are too hard so I don't like them.

Most food has a horrible texture. Like mashed potato for example. It is like paper which has been soaked in water. It feels like papier mâché which might go into every crevice of my mouth like a sculpture. It's bit strange but I seem to have the best appetite for food and drink when I have just brushed my teeth.

I don't like restaurants at all, especially when people stay for ages chatting and eating and it can sometimes be so disgusting I can't stay there at all.

 Also they hardly ever have anything I like. Sometimes I might ask for a bowl of grated cheese but then they give me Cheddar instead of Red Leicester. Or else it's not grated finely enough. It would be better if they sold Pringles or Cadbury's chocolate in restaurants.

Touch

Some things which feel really good to touch are playdough and beeswax. I liked to play with these a lot at the Steiner School. I also like the feel of very smooth stones like some of the ones you might find on the beach. Another good one is the feel of the underside of the leaves of some plants.

In my mouth I like the feel of Pringles best because they are noisy and crunchy, and I quite like drinking through a straw. I also like the feeling of the electric tooth brush in my mouth and the rubber gloves in the dentist.

One of the reasons I love my sleeping bag so much is because of how nice it feels against my skin. I love to get right inside it and draw it tight. It is a lovely soft feel, not like some of the horrible, plasticky-feeling sleeping bags you can get. Sometimes I curl up happily in my sleeping bag in all parts of the house, even the kitchen floor!

The very best feeling of all is Sandy's fur. Sandy is such a cute cat. (Being 'a cute' cat doesn't mean he is less than 90 degrees by the way!)

I just love to stroke him and stroke him every moment of the day. When he was younger I used to wish he would stay still for two minutes sometimes. Quite often I let Sandy into my room with me. He's a lot calmer now than he used to be and this has helped me too. You can learn a lot about relaxing from watching a cat!

Sometimes Sandy hides inside my sleeping bag. I love to hold him and rub my cheek against his fur. This is the best feeling in the whole world. It is much better than *any* fabric. I hate rough fabrics against my skin, for example wool and I don't like labels sticking into my skin. One excellent fabric is soft cotton. I have a blue T-shirt which is 100 per cent cotton and it feels excellent against my skin so I like to wear it a lot. I don't like silk — it is too soft, like a fake softness.

One thing I hate to see is when cats or dogs wear those wee coats made of some fabric. I mean, a cat might even wear a rainbow colour coat. The natural colours of cats are far better. I hate to see dogs wearing those wee coats too. They already have lovely fur coats. When I see a cat or dog wearing a coat that a human has put on them it makes me mad. It reminds me of a wet suit on them. If humans wear a wet suit that is OK because it's their choice and after all they have all that water fun to look forward to.

I like being alone

This is another unusual thing about me. I prefer being on my own a lot of the time and I hate crowds big time. I'm also not keen on strangers coming into my house. One thing which upsets me is the noise of the chatter when there are a lot of people together. If I am upset about something being alone helps.

One of my favourite places in the world is Rathlin Island. This is a very quiet place. Not very many people live there, and visitors are not allowed to bring any cars onto the island. I'm not sure exactly but I think there are only about six children on the whole island. I visit there each year. That is a place I might like to live when I grow up. There are plenty of species of seabirds to see there like puffins for example and you can see them from a high cliff. I like birds. We have plenty in our garden and my favourite is the robin.

The best place in the world for me is my room and I hate anyone to come in without knocking. I have a bird feeder outside my bedroom window. My room is very high up so no cats can reach there.

Sometimes I curl myself up like a wee hedgehog inside my sleeping bag. At the weekend or on days off the thing I love to do best is to spend the whole day in my jammies and sleeping bag. I love that. One thing I love about my sleeping bag is that it feels nice and soft and gentle. When I am in it I feel happy.

I also love reading or playing on my own in my room. A good career for me when I grow up might be a book publisher, because you could spend your time reading and rating books. One thing I would have to remember is that not everybody likes the same books I do. I might work for a publishing company when I grow up. This is one possibility. But I've thought of lots of things I might do like be an athlete or a footballer or a Formula One racing driver. I even thought of a sleeping bag tester. There must be sleeping bag testers who would try out sleeping bags and rate them for cosiness, but I don't think they have chocolate testers. I'll just have to wait and see.

My ideas

Another thing I have a lot of fun doing in my room is planning things and making up ideas in my head. There are lots of ideas. Like planning to start a pop group. It would be called 'The Friendlies' and have my favourite cuddly toys in it. They are Bugs, Baby Panda and Sam.

Gaelica is another of my ideas. Gaelica is the name of my kingdom which is mostly in my room at present. Gaelica is better than this country because there is peace there. In Gaelica I am king but I am not superior. No-one is superior. In Gaelica there are very strict safety standards but no territories. When Neil came, I let him be the prime minister so he could make up the rules. Neil is my best friend and he is the person who understands me best in the world. He and I are very very similar. We think the same things are fun. But he lives far away. I wish he lived nearer so then I could see him more often.

Another of my ideas is the Portal. Sometimes I have been able to enter a parallel solar system by going through a portal in the hall. When I went there I swapped bodies temporarily with a boy called Ken. Although he looked exactly like me he was not really me. It was Ken. He came to my house while I went off to his planet.

My Mum knew for sure it was not me because I hate being called Ken instead of Kenneth. Ken was the exact opposite of me. For example he loved eating and handwriting and was hopeless at maths. Mum said that while Ken was here maybe he could eat up Kenneth's lunch.

Where Ken comes from everything is the wrong way round. We live in a steep valley, and my Mum is on a diet to put on lots of weight. Ken hates maths. The kids start off doing three-dimensional trigonometry and make their way to adding two plus two. The fridge is used for microwaving things and the microwave oven is for cooling them down. Where Ken lives Sandy is a horrible dog instead of the cutest wee cat in the world. But then we like horrible dogs because everything is back to front. And Chris is an evil step father who spends his time putting bugs onto people's computers.

It's a really weird place. I nearly got stuck there but the portal is closed now.

My worries

At night I usually don't get to sleep till very late. When I try I find there are too many thoughts going on in my head. Sometimes I find myself going into Worry World. I worry about a lot of things. Like the time I swallowed a bit of plastic – I was petrified for weeks about that. Another time there had been a wasp's nest in the garden. I was convinced there were some wasps in my room somewhere. I might also worry about what would happen if there was a fire, or what I should do as a career when I grow up.

It's a bit strange, but sometimes I don't know what I am worried about. I just know I am worried and I can't tell what it is about. There are so many possibilities of things which might happen.

One thing which can happen on this planet is a disaster. Disaster can happen at any moment without warning and I worry about this. There could be a volcano or an earthquake. These are natural disasters.

The Omagh bombing was a man-made disaster. The people thought the bomb was somewhere else and ended up getting bombed. Wars and battles are also man-made disasters where thousands of people get killed. Sometimes there are a lot of war crimes where ordinary citizens are attacked even though you are only supposed to attack soldiers in a war.

These days people are
learning ways to find
peace. People are learning
a bit better. Where I live in
Northern Ireland there
has been war for a long
time. At the moment there
is a cease-fire. But there
are always problems. In
the future I hope I can tell my kids about this and
they won't even believe me, it is so stupid. The two
sides are Catholics and Protestants. If the world was
really Christian there would not be any wars or
fighting each other. Fighting is not true Christianity.

I don't go to school

Not going to school is definitely an unusual thing
about me. Most kids go to school. This is because
most kids learn the same way and like being
together.

I went to two different schools when I was
younger. First was the primary school. I hate to
think about this. I didn't learn much at school at all.
I prefer to teach myself. And anyway being in a
group only puts me off. The best way for me to learn

is one-to-one or else on my own through reading and computers.

In school there are lots of desks in rows and kids are supposed to stay at their desks and learn the things the way the teacher tells them. Then at lunch and break time they have free time when they don't have to stay at their desks. At these times they often break into groups. Sometimes these groups argue with each other. The worst thing to be is a neutral kid. I was a neutral kid when I was at school. I didn't like being part of any group. School can be tough on neutral kids.

Also I really hated the playground. This was because the other kids said things to me too mean to repeat. Also it was very noisy and it was hard to find a quiet corner anywhere.

The Rudolf Steiner School was nicer and the teacher was much kinder to me. But I still didn't like doing the same as the others and the groups spoiled it. The chatter noise was hard to put up with. It was a bit better for a while when she put my desk apart from the others.

Sometimes Jacinta asked me to help some of the others with their reading for a while, but this got a bit boring. One thing I always used to do at school was to make sure I was the very last one to leave the classroom. I did this every single day without fail. I got very upset if anyone tried to change this on me.

I was glad when Mum decided to keep me at home. This was soon after we discovered about my AS and since then my life has changed completely.

How I learn

Autism means having an unusual brain, so I have an unusual way of learning. Some things I didn't have to learn, like reading, because I just knew how without being taught. Some things I can learn very quickly as long as it's not pointless and the way I am taught is right. Some things I have to work very hard at. I usually use ABA for these things. When people have to try hard to learn something that is called applying yourself.

One of the best ways to learn new things is through reading. I love reading and I learn a lot this way. I think you can definitely learn more through reading than TV. But I love TV, especially the

Disney Channel. Except I think lots of things on TV are not at all suitable for children.

Sometimes I have a very good memory for things I have learned, especially when I have read them. I definitely remember things best when I read them. Sometimes I see my thoughts. Sometimes I find it very hard to concentrate. Especially when I am asked to do things which are pointless. I find it extremely difficult to remember what I am supposed to be doing sometimes.

I also have some special gifts. These are things I can do like a much older kid, like reading and maths. And I was made a member of Mensa because of the high IQ result. I got quite a nice personal membership card with my name on it, but apart from that I can't say Mensa is very interesting for children.

Words and reading

I have always been interested in words. One unusual thing is that when people speak to me I see the text of the words they are saying and when I read words I hear them inside my head. I love the jokes you can make with words and I make these jokes a lot.

Here are some good jokes I might make:

When I overheard my Mum say she would 'take that with a pinch of salt' I gave her some pepper and said – sorry, that was all I could find!

And when she said she was ordering some goods by mail order I said – I don't see why you don't try fe-mail order.

When I heard the word optimum used I said – 'How come it's up to mum and not up to dad?'

When I got green ink on my fingers I said I must be a good gardener.

Once a drink got spilt and I said: 'At least it was a dry sherry!'

What do you call it when you trust a fat man? Giving the benefit of the stout!

Another one is:

What do you call a famous detective who is also an estate agent?
Sherlock Homes!

Another funny thing I like is practical jokes. I do tricks sometimes. Like once I put fake scratches on Chris's car and he thought it was real. And once I put trick soap in the bathroom which made my Mum's face all black, and she didn't know why I was laughing. I have tricked people, including Ken Kerr, with fake biscuits as well. Ken Kerr took two and he thought they were a bit off at first. This was good fun. And I love Peter Sellers films. These are hilarious. Clowns are fun. I can do some quite funny clown acts myself.

Reading is not work at all for me – it is one of my very favourite things to do in the world. I read an awful lot and I read very quickly as well. When I was tested my reading age was 17, which was very unusual.

When I first started school the other kids were learning how to read but I already knew how. I had already discovered how when I was very young. The teacher was teaching us very easy words like 'Look, Book'. I didn't understand why she was doing this, because I didn't realise reading was so different for me. I had already read some really good books, like the Narnia Chronicles before I went to school. I have read them stacks of times since then. I love the Narnia Chronicles. C.S. Lewis is one of my favourite authors.

Reading was one of the few good things about primary school. I used to read all the books very quickly. Sometimes the teacher gave me extra reading to do. Sometimes she wanted me to answer comprehension questions on it, but I didn't because it was boring and pointless and I hate doing boring, pointless things. The teacher tried to get me to write and answer questions about some things the same as the other kids. But I didn't want to so I refused.

While I was at the Steiner School I read tons of books. One of my very favourite books then was 'Danny, the Champion of the World' by Roald Dahl and Jacinta let me read this over and over.

Up on the wall Jacinta had a list with all the children's names and the books from the school library that they had read. I had read them all so here is what she put for me:

> *Name — Kenneth.*
>
> *Books read — Every book!*

Maths

Maths is something I can understand easily, which is why I have done my GCSE in maths. Here's how it all happened.

It was really because of Jacinta at the start. I didn't do much maths while I was at school because of all the problems like groups and handwriting and boredom and noise. Nobody even knew about my maths gift before Jacinta found out. I am not sure how exactly she found out but when she did she told the Education Board all about it.

Then the Education Board sent people out to do some tests. I can't remember any of them very well except Julie Connell. She checked out my maths ability and then she told Mum I was off the chart. Then Mum gave me some maths to do at home for age 12 which was quite interesting.

But Mum didn't know that much about maths so she got herself a GCSE maths book so she could learn it herself. One day she was on the phone for ages. This is one thing which definitely annoys me, so I read the GCSE book. When she came back off the phone Mum was annoyed because I had overtaken the place she was at. I was really annoyed too because she wouldn't believe I had read it all. She wanted me to write things down and repeat things and I refused because it was pointless and boring. In the end she realised I had understood it OK and said I could go on ahead at my own pace. After that I soon got all the GCSE book read myself.

The Education Board were very pleased with me for doing so well and they said I could go ahead and sit the GCSE exam six years ahead of time. This is really cool because it will save me a lot of trouble when I am older. Then before I did the exam Julie May helped me with my maths book 'GCSE Revision in a Week'.

What I would say about the GCSE exam is that it was not very tricky but not easy either. And that I definitely wouldn't have done so well if I had not worked. This shows that you can work at things and get better even if you have a gift.

This photo was in the paper when I passed my GCSE maths

Some maths is very interesting. For example I am extremely interested in Pi because no-one has yet found out its exact value. I read a book all about Pi. It is supposed to go on forever. This is an example of infinity. Lots of people have investigated it for thousands of years. Fifty-one billion digits are known at present.

The one millionth digit of Pi is the digit one. I bet you didn't know that!

How I feel about being different

I can't say how much of my difference is because of my AS because AS is part of me and there's no way of knowing what I would be like without it. But it is definitely a good thing that everyone is different, because otherwise it would be a very boring world.

I don't remember any time when I didn't know I was different, but when I was younger I didn't understand how I was different. I just thought I was normal and everyone else was different.

We didn't find out about AS till I was eight and then Mum told me about it. I have a half-clear, half-vague memory of when she told me. I remember we got started off on ABA right away because we had a lot of work to do on my behaviour.

It was very tough when I didn't understand what it was that was different about me. I got blamed for lots of things and people were very unfair. Mum thought I was just badly behaved. This can happen a lot to AS kids.

I don't fully understand what AS is. Nobody knows for sure and it is very hard to explain. I know there was a guy called Asperger who was interested in kids like me.

I like being different. I would prefer being different to being normal. I am glad to have AS and I am proud of who I am.

Chapter Three

My Strengths

Honesty

I think honesty is a very important strength. The world would probably be better if people were more honest. I like people to be honest and say what they mean. AS kids are very truthful. Honesty is one of the best parts about AS – maybe the very best. I am always completely honest to everyone. I don't tell lies.

I like other people being honest and saying what they mean. And I like people keeping promises. Sometimes you have to be careful with honesty. For example if a 790lb lady asked if she was fat then you would say yes, but you might have to run for it. I suppose you wouldn't have to run very far if she was very fat.

Here are some of the things I am always honest about:

If I am unhappy about something I tell the truth. Like if I am fed up with a visitor. Or if I dislike something. Or if I dislike a person. Or if someone does or says something stupid. Or makes a mistake.

If I don't want to do something then I will be honest and I will probably refuse to do it. For example if work is pointless and boring then I refuse to do it. Like repeating sums or doing corrections.

Once Lorna tried and tried to get me to write answers to comprehension questions on a (true!) newspaper article about a head-teacher who banned Harry Potter books from her school. I completely refused to do this on the grounds that I had no interest whatsoever in such a stupid, brainless person. I don't know how such a person ever got to be a head-teacher. And I hate handwriting anyway.

Sometimes adults get annoyed when I am honest.

Personality

One of my very best strengths is that I work extremely hard at my AS difficulties and I have put a lot of effort in since we found out about my AS.

Everyone has a different personality. One thing about me is that I am absolutely determined to be myself and I will not let anyone try to change me. I know my own mind and like to go my own way and do my own thing. For example I would really hate it if anyone tried to make me into a non-AS kid. If they tried, I would probably feel like grabbing the nearest heavy thing I could manage to lift and hitting them with it.

As well as gifts I also have challenges and it is the challenges which make me strong. These are the things I find difficult, and I have to work very hard at them. I am very determined to work very hard on the difficulties. I am always up for a challenge which is good, because taking on challenges can make you very strong.

I have a positive attitude to AS now but I didn't always have a positive attitude at all. What changed was that things became more positive around me. People have treated me better since we found out about my AS. Some of my difficulties have made me stronger and wiser. When you have AS there are a lot of situations where being strong really helps. If I explain some of these situations then this book could be very useful.

ABA

Another thing I have learnt a lot about is ABA. When you have AS you have to make a lot of effort to learn about how to behave. This takes a lot of hard work. ABA is something which has helped me a lot.

I know quite a few ABA experts. Emma is one ABA therapist I see a lot. We have a lot of fun together. The only other one whose name I can remember is Ken Kerr. He is a man with a beard who helps me with some of my difficulties. He is kind and helpful. He is quite a famous world expert on ABA. Once I got a certificate from him because of how well I did in my ABA work.

I have done really well with ABA. Once I was even on TV because of how well I had done with ABA. I have used it for learning stacks of things. ABA is all about challenges and that is why it helps me so much. It has worked well for a lot of things but it hasn't worked for eating yet.

I would definitely recommend ABA for any kid. For a start kids are not punished. They are encouraged instead. In our house we use a Token Economy. How this works is that I can earn tokens for good behaviour or get fined for bad behaviour. The tokens are really plastic money which stops them getting mixed up with real money.

In the hall we have a special cupboard called the ABA cupboard which keeps all the ABA stuff together. I help Mum with ABA ideas a lot. For example if I see something in a mail-order catalogue which looks cool then I tell Mum so she can get it for the ABA store. We always have a discussion if there are going to be any rule changes. Sometimes I give her ideas for fairer rules. Sometimes when I make up a rule which makes things more difficult for me she says she is glad I am a very honest boy.

At the moment we keep a special ABA Behaviour Notebook. How this works is that every day I get awarded Happy Faces ☺ or Sad Faces ☹ for my behaviour throughout the whole day.

Here are some of the of things I might get Happy Faces for:

- ☺ Eating,
- ☺ Being obedient, for example getting my jammies on when I am asked,
- ☺ Being friendly,
- ☺ Being helpful for example feeding Sandy,
- ☺ Being pleasant and polite,
- ☺ Taking a shower,
- ☺ Respecting authority,
- ☺ Making a special effort.

I can get Double Happy Faces ☺ ☺ for when I do something good without anyone asking or reminding me.

Here are some of the things I might get Sad Faces for:

- ☹ Not doing as I am told,

☹ Shouting,

☹ Being cheeky or rude or unpleasant,

☹ Arguing,

☹ Not eating,

☹ Ignoring people,

☹ Correcting people.

Mostly these days I get Happy Faces for doing good things because my behaviour has improved so much!

At the end of the day we calculate the day's score and I convert it into a percentage. This decides how many tokens I have earned. For example if I get 100 per cent Happy Faces for the day this earns me a full 100 tokens.

The maximum I could usually earn in one day is 100 tokens. But there are bonuses available sometimes for special things. For three bonuses I can get a Lucky Dip. A Lucky Dip is when tickets for some of the prizes are put into a container and one is drawn out.

Mum has stacks of ABA prizes stashed away in the ABA cupboard in the hall and in her room under the bed which I can save for. I can save up for any prize at all, but I am not allowed to buy ABA prizes with real money because that would be too easy.

The kind of prizes I can get are books, posters, comics, sweets and games. There is a token price for each one which is the same as the real money price.

Challenges and things which have helped

I think a lot of AS kids could do really well with challenges. The most difficult kind of challenge is to do something you really hate to do or find very difficult. Chris always tells me effort is what matters, and challenges help here because they encourage me to make my best effort.

Since we found out about my AS I have taken on stacks of things. Handwriting was one of the first things we did with ABA but I can't remember much about what we did at the start. I remember we used a timer and prizes. I still hate handwriting but ABA helped me tons.

Since we started I have worked on lots of other things and I have definitely made good progress. I know I have still hundreds more things to work on but I am determined to do my best.

Anger

I have done a lot of work on anger. It is easy for me to get angry about a lot of things. I had to learn a lot about this and it was a big challenge for me. I used to get really angry if things didn't go my way.

One day I went to see Leo. (She is a very kind doctor.) There was a problem just before we left the house. Mum and I had been playing chess and I lost. Usually I win, so I was very annoyed. I wanted to go back a few moves or else have another game, but Mum refused. She said we were going to be late.

I got very, very angry. What I did was to complain and argue and refuse to leave and shout loudly and throw a lot of things around. For example I threw toys and furniture. Anything I could find really. In fact if a high up window had been open then the most valuable breakable things would have been out of it.

I had calmed down a lot when we got to Leo's but I completely ignored Mum and Leo at first and didn't listen to a word they said. In the end Leo got out a flipchart and I did a lot of drawings about what had happened and how I felt. Then we discussed it and we came up a lot of really good ideas. I did a lot of drawings (which are in this book now) of good and bad ways to behave when you feel angry.

I have made really good progress on anger. I can't help getting angry sometimes, but I have learned a lot and tried very hard. I usually deal with it a lot better these days.

ANGER THERAPY SECTION

Here is the list I made at Leo's that day:

AAAAGGGHH!!!!!!! I'M ANGRY!!!!!!!

Do's

Punch a punchbag

Draw funny pictures

Pummel a pillow

Talk

Have a joke

Walk

ANGER THERAPY SECTION

Don't's

Hit people

Suppress it

Throw things

Sulk

Shout at people

Tease

Here are examples of some of my other challenges and how I am getting on with them:

Obedience

One of my main problems used to be misbehaving and hardly ever doing what I was told. The reason for this was that I couldn't see the point. Sometimes it's hard to know what is expected so I like it when things are clearly explained and there are very clear and fair rules and I behave best then. I think this is because I know exactly what is expected from me.

Before we found out about my AS I used to have a much bigger problem with my behaviour. Being obedient was a pretty rare thing back then. I hated not being able to do just what I wanted so there was no reason to be obedient. This caused a lot of problems. Then when we started ABA I started having a reason to be obedient. Like earning tokens for example. Now I am much more obedient and a lot happier.

Accepting authority

When adults give children long lectures about authority this is usually quite boring. Authority is something I have always found hard to understand. It is difficult to see the reason why children have to do what older people tell us. Just because they have been on the planet longer than children. I mean that's not the children's fault, is it? I have never liked this idea at all.

This used to cause a lot of problems with me being cheeky and then getting an hour long lecture from Mum. But I understand it better now. I know that adults can be wiser and smarter than children and that it is good for children to learn to accept authority. And it is also one good way of earning tokens!

One thing I have worked hard on is drama therapy work with Kate or Julie May or Mum. Sometimes in drama with Mum we do a role play situation where I am a very spoilt cheeky brat who won't do anything I am told at all and I want everything my own way. A bit like Draco Malfoy from the Harry Potter books. Mum plays a harassed mother who completely spoils me to try and get me to keep quiet. This can be really good fun. In role plays you can be as cheeky as you like and you won't get into any trouble!

Making mistakes

Before I knew I had AS I used to get really upset when I made a mistake. A lot of kids with AS get upset when they make mistakes and I know how that feels. I am learning to deal with mistakes better but I still do not like making mistakes.

Here's a very important and useful thing which my grandpa used to say: 'The man who never made a mistake never made anything.'

Making mistakes can be very difficult for me but I have worked hard at this difficulty. When I made mistakes here are some of the things I did:

- shout loudly,
- refuse to continue,
- throw down my pencil,
- say it was someone else's fault,
- say it must be a typing error.

I can't remember exactly how I felt when I did these things except that I was very angry. I think that this was because I felt so awful. I felt as if I was stupid.

Chris has taught me a lot of wise things which have helped me to accept making mistakes. For example, he taught me that mistakes are learning opportunities. I reckon this does not mean we necessarily learn from mistakes, but they are one way of learning. Chris has a good motto:

'Mistakes are cool!'

When he says this I feel as if I am not stupid even though I have made a mistake.

I also read a very helpful book all about mistakes that worked. In 1930 a lady called Ruth Wakefield was baking and she ran out of chocolate. So, instead, she put chocolate chips into the dough. She thought they would melt. Instead she invented chocolate chip cookies by mistake!

So you have got to look out for ways of learning from mistakes because there is always a possibility. This is a wise and intelligent thing to do.

Speaking clearly and not interrupting

I used to not speak very clearly at all. Mum and I made up the Clear Speech Game. This became really famous. Ken Kerr was so impressed with us he even put it on the Internet and into his book about ABA.

The Clear Speech Game helped with the difficulty with interrupting too. I know I have definitely made progress with interrupting, because I used to find it extremely difficult not to interrupt, and now I only find it moderately difficult.

Wanting attention

This is something I still find extremely difficult and I still need to work on. I still have hundreds of things to work on.

How it feels when I want attention and don't get it is still really bad. Even worse than extremely angry. I feel almost like attacking someone so as to get attention.

Being pleasant

This is another difficult one. Without a lot of help it can be impossible to be pleasant. For example if you say something funny it can be the wrong time sometimes. Instead of funny it can be cheeky, rude, critical or sarcastic. It can be hard to know when comments are funny and when they are not OK. When they are not OK people are going to react badly.

Relaxing

Recently I have been making a lot of effort to learn to relax, and this is a very important challenge. It can be very difficult to relax. But relaxation is a very useful thing to learn and it is helping me a lot. I am finding it so helpful that I told Mum she should have got to work on relaxation right at the start, just as soon as we found out about my AS.

Nowadays I do a lot of relaxation work. I have learnt lots of ways to relax. Some of my best techniques are listening to relaxation tapes or pummelling a cuddly toy like Leo. Or having Deep Pressure Therapy. Or music. Or art.

Deep Pressure Therapy is what I call it when I lie inside the sleeping bag and Mum gets the Peanut Roll and rolls it right over me, leaning as heavily as possible. The harder the better. Somehow for me the feeling of being squashed or squeezed tight is brilliant. When I get the Deep Pressure Therapy in the evening here's how I sleep that night – Not like a log. Not even like a tree. But like *all* the trees in the forest!

I have found other excellent ways to relax like stroking Sandy, or reading, or going for a walk beside the sea.

Tension is the opposite of relaxation. When I am tense I like to be on my own for long times. A lot of things make me tense but I am not sure exactly what these things are.

GCSE maths was not the kind of thing I find too difficult so I was not too tense for this at all. In fact I was quite relaxed. I did a practical joke on Julie May just before I started the exam by offering her a nut from a trick tin of nuts. When she opened the tin a big snake popped out and made a loud noise. This was really funny. I think the adults were more tense than me that day.

Here is an excellent technique which I made up to avoid exam stress: think about something else and do as many relaxing things as you can think of close to the exam. Like go for a walk, or maybe art therapy or music therapy or Deep Pressure Therapy. Then the split second before the exam starts think about the exam *and nothing else.* This worked really well for me.

Swimming

Another relaxing thing I have learnt to do is swimming. I learnt this through ABA. Mum took me on my own every day while I was learning. I earned a lot of tokens for learning to swim.

Each day we made the goal more difficult. I started off with just getting into the water. At first I had two arm bands and two floats. Then one arm band. Then no arm bands. Then two floats. Then one float. Then no floats.

Then I did one stroke out to Mum and back to the edge. Then two strokes, then three and so on. Right up till I was half-way across. In the end all the way across. This was after a few weeks. Now I can swim really well. The arm bit was always the difficult bit for me. I have very powerful legs. This is why I run and twirl round a lot. I can even swim right across the pool with my hands held tightly behind my back.

I enjoy swimming now. I only like to go at times when it's very empty, like when other kids are at school. One difficulty with swimming is that I hate a crowded pool and I hate the changing room.

Music

I also enjoy any kind of music, especially ABBA (this is nothing to do with ABA). All their songs are great. I like most types of music, and at the moment I am learning to play Grade 1 on the piano.

I have also tried music therapy. It is excellent fun. You can do any instrument, or sing or dance. I am starting it again soon and I can hardly wait.

Art

My favourite type of painting is done by using watercolour on a really large sheet. In tutoring a few weeks ago I made a big display about the sea. This had a sea painting. My display went up on the noticeboard in Crawfords-

burn Countryside Centre. Sometimes I also draw stick pictures.

Another excellent thing is cross-stitch. I love doing cross-stitch. You can do pattern or freehand and make beautiful designs. I have been good at cross-stitch since I was quite small. With cross-stitch you can make lovely book marks or you can have the work framed and put on the wall.

I used to do art therapy with Anne Marie who died. She was a very kind Dutch lady. We were good friends and I miss her sometimes. I enjoyed art therapy. It is not just painting. It's every type of art – painting, drawing, modelling. Modelling is excellent. I modelled lots of animals and they all had names, but I can't remember all the names now.

Being organised

Sometimes I find it extremely hard to be organised. I quite often forget what I am supposed to be doing. Like if Mum asks me to go and get my shoes on, I usually come back ten minutes later and ask what was I supposed to be doing. So it can be difficult to be organised. But I like things to be organised so that I know exactly what's going on and where things are. For example, I hate people to move any of my belongings. I like to have them where I want them. I hate it when some one tidies my room on me (notice I said *on* me not *for* me!).

I like to be in charge of things and know what's going on and when it's happening. It is helpful when Mum writes out the day's plans. One thing which was quite useful was when Mum made me an organiser with a daily schedule. We have a laminator and we use it for a lot of things which help me. She made lots of laminated cards we could stick on with velcro. This showed what had to be done and in what order. There were cards for Free Time and fun activities too. It can be helpful to see what is happening when and if there are any choices.

One day I put three schedule cards in a row: PlayStation, PlayStation, PlayStation. Mum let me get away with it! She is a lot softer at the weekend. One day when she went out I organised my schedule myself. I chose an Outing Card and we went for an outing to Seahill. We walked along the sea. It was good because we hardly met any people. Mum got very cold but I was OK.

Another good tip for being organised is to remember this motto: 'A Place for Everything and Everything in its Own Place.'

I have this motto on the notice board in my room.

Organising this book

Getting a book organised can be quite difficult really. Here's how this one got started. One day Julie Connell was at our house and she came up with the idea of me writing a book. At the start it was going to be a book to help the Edu-   cation Board explain about Asperger Syndrome. It was for helping people in schools. Because a lot of people don't know much about AS and she said I might be able to help explain it.

I said it was a good idea. To help get me organised at the start she sent out a student called Michelle once a week. Michelle helped me by using index cards. First I had to decide all my section headings and have an index card for each one. This meant that all the information and ideas could be sorted into their proper sections. Later on I opened folders on the laptop for them all instead. At the end Mum used ABA to encourage me to get it finished off.

I really liked it at the start when Michelle came because we used to have great fun playing Table Top Football together.

A good thing about the book is that it might help people with AS with ideas about how to work on their difficulties. You see there are lots of undiagnosed people. In fact everybody has at least some autism.

Some of the things that are said about people with AS are not true at all. I bet people with autism could do a lot of things really well if they just get help with things like organising and relaxing. For example, they say that AS people prefer factual books to fiction. Personally I prefer fiction stories any day. I make up fictional ideas in my head a lot but I don't usually write them down. Dawn persuaded me to write this one down.

Here is a fictional story written by me:

That shrinking feeling

Break time. The kitchen smells funny. Hazel's been using bleach. Mum's gone to answer the phone. Dawn and I are sipping tea. I feel very strange. The world seems to be enlarging. No, it's me getting smaller.

'Heeeelllllp!'

'Dawn, quickly, come here. What's happened to us?'

'I'm not sure, but it looks like we've shrunk.'

'Either that or we need new glasses.'

Mum's just walked in.

'Dawn, look out!'

'Quick, let's get out of here before we get walked on'

STOMP!

'Phew, that was close.'

'Dawn, there's a gap under the door, quick let's go!!'

In the conservatory now. Safe.

'Let's hitch a ride on the cat's back, Dawn. It'll take us out to the garden.'

'This is better now, Kenneth. At least we'll be safe out here.'

Just then we find an old newspaper. The headline says: 'POISONOUS FUMES IN BLEACH!'

'So that's what happened, Dawn.'

'Kenneth, look at all those ants. Let's follow them.'

Just then we come to a racing track for worms (ridden by ants). I decide to enter the race.

I put two sugar cubes and one sweet on me winning the race at 100 to 1 odds. I jump on the worm's saddle.

The commentator says 'The flag's up now and they're off! Kenneth's in the lead, it looks like he might win this. He's half way already, no, three quar... he's won!'

Dawn collects my packet of sugar cubes and packet of sweets and asks the ants to look after it.

Meanwhile the worm backs me into the pond and a fish tries to eat me, but pushes me closer to the surface each time. Just before I get to the top, a dragonfly lifts me to safety.

Dawn and I decide to explore. We discover Patio Airport. There are lots of butterfly planes. We see a ladybird jet for sale. Unfortunately my winnings are in ant money, and this land belongs to grasshoppers. So I get it changed.

We use the money to buy the ladybird jet and fly through an open window just before the effect wears off.

The End

Chapter Four

My Beliefs

I do a lot of thinking about things which interest me and I have strong views about many things, like crime for example. I am dead against crime.

Here are some of my thoughts and opinions:

Gifts

A gift is something you are given, so it is good to be thankful for gifts. My family and my cat are some of the best gifts in my life. There are many gifts in life. In fact life is full of gifts, but lots of them are wasted because most people are too blind to see them as gifts. The most important gifts to receive are probably peace and wisdom.

Some gifts are for everyone to share. Nature gives many gifts each day. Things like trees and flowers and birds and sunsets.

Sometimes people boast about their gifts because they want to seem better than other people. Boasting is mean and stupid and selfish. All people have unique gifts. Like the ability to do certain things very well. I mean some people are better runners than others. Some people are better cooks. You just have to work with your talents.

Some of my gifts are special because they are unusual. It would be terrible to receive a special gift and instead of saying 'thankyou' saying 'that's not enough, I want more'. So I am glad of my gifts.

Intelligence

One of my gifts is intelligence. Intelligence on this planet usually means you can work out things. Like angles in a circle for example. But real intelligence is when you face a difficult situation wisely.

Kindness is far more important than intelligence anyway but people often do not realise this. Kindness is not respected. People give too much respect to people who are very smart or wealthy. Pop stars for example. What they do is to sing songs, like ABBA. They get a lot of fame. Thousands of people sometimes go

to their concerts and so they make a lot of money. Many people have more money than they need, but others have not enough. Like people in the Third World.

The Third World is the name for the part of the world that is quite undeveloped. People there do not have enough food. This is not because there is not enough food in the world but because it is not fairly divided up. This is a difficult problem.

Something I am very interested in is wisdom. Wisdom is far more important than intelligence really. Humans think intelligence is more important but what is the use of knowing things like how many degrees are in a triangle if you are not a wise person. Wisdom helps you deal with difficult situations.

I would like to be wise. Wanting to be wise is the first step to becoming wise. This means I have already taken the first step in the right direction, just by wanting to be wise. It also means anyone at all can become wise if they want to.

Nature

I am a great nature lover. I love to go on quiet nature rambles and I love to see lovely views which are untouched by man.

The most beautiful things to see are part of nature. I love looking at beautiful things – for example the way God makes the pond look beautiful even in the rain, with all the moving circles. I also like to look at the colours in a sunset. Sometimes people miss the beautiful things.

I hate the way humans disrespect the environment. I hate to see plastics being used which do not rot. Rotting is part of nature's way of keeping the earth healthy. Some things can never be replaced and it is stupid to ignore this.

I also hate to see people dropping litter. Sometimes they do this even where there is a warning notice.

Animals

I greatly admire and respect all living creatures. Especially my pet cat, Sandy. I love him a lot – I adore the way he is soft and furry and when I got him it was the happiest day of my life.

Sometimes I dream of being in the animal kingdom where the birds and rabbits have stalls and markets. Animals are really very intelligent, but humans don't often see this. If I were in the animal kingdom I'd like to be a bird. It would be cool to be able to fly. I wouldn't like the migrating part, though. I could be a robin. I could stay at home all year round and have a great feast round the window sill. It would be cool to see my photo on all those Christmas cards!

Once I had a hamster called Snowy. This was not as good as having a pet cat. I think cats have ESP (extra sensory perception). I think my cat is the cutest wee thing in the world (I say this all the time) even though sometimes he bites and scrabs a bit. When he does this I can never stay cross with him for long – probably about two seconds maximum. I always make sure that any food we leave out for the birds is well away from the cats.

I believe all creatures are the greatest in their own way and I believe all animals are equal. Humans like to think they are the smartest and the greatest creatures but they are not. Have you ever heard of another creature so dumb that it drops bombs on each other, or hunts other creatures just for *fun*? Why do they not get punished for this? I believe no innocent creature should be harmed. Animals don't start wars or destroy the planet.

I hate a lot of things about the way humans treat animals. Who do humans think they are to mistreat animals? I hate to see that. I hate hunting because it is just killing animals for sport. I dislike meat eating. It is not necessary to eat meat. I am a vegetarian which means I don't eat any meat. But then I don't eat any vegetables or fruit either. So I suppose I am more of a Pringle-arian.

I hate animal cruelty. People who are cruel to their pets ought to be jailed instead of just stopped from owning another animal. I hate to hear of animals becoming extinct. This is usually the fault of humans being stupid, burning up so much fuel and destroying the atmosphere.

Let this be a lesson to all you guys who are scoffing up food or else burning up fuel as you read this – STOP! THINK! Do you really want your children to live in a world with practically no ozone layer?

Churches and fighting

People should respect other people's religions. I dislike churches not being friendly with each other. Churches should not be fighting with each other if

they are genuine churches. They should just say: 'We've got different opinions but that does not make either of us evil.' They should sort these things out peacefully. Fighting is not true Christianity.

Sometimes I wonder how Jesus felt when He was nailed to the cross. I reckon He felt very happy. He would have felt great pain of course, but the happiness of doing God's will would overcome that pain.

The media

Sometimes I get really upset about the media. It makes me angry that there is so little time on TV for kids. Adults are very selfish – all those hours for adult programmes. Another thing is that you can't even trust the rating system. For example, some things which are supposed to be suitable for kids are not. There is too much exposure on TV of three kinds – physical, mental and spiritual. Those programs are what I call corrupt. By physical exposure I mean things like nudity. Things like the Ricky Lake show are mental exposure. These encourage people to talk about private things on TV. They also encourage people to take each other for granted. The programme about the Protestant and Catholic families who live next door to each other is a very bad thing. This just makes the problems worse.

Some people might never like those corrupt programs even when they are over eighteen. They could not look at that kind of thing no matter what age they were. That is nothing to ashamed of. I think that is something to be proud of. But if children went to the government to protest about these things they would not be taken seriously because they are children. In Northern Ireland they are trying to start a Minister for Children in the new government which is a good thing.

I reckon the voting age should be lowered anyway, eighteen is way too old. Kids could make just as good a choice as adults. Maybe ten or eleven would be better. Though not five year olds. I don't think they would really be interested in voting.

Here are my favourite four channels on TV: Disney Channel, Disney Channel, Disney Channel, and then any other channel! Disney has eighteen hours per day of programmes for kids, which is excellent.

The news

The news on TV tells us about all over the world but information about the past we have to get from history books. The news on TV is usually bad news. The good way of looking at this is that bad things happen much more rarely than good things. So good things are not interesting enough to go onto the news.

Gravity and dimensions

Gravity is an invisible force pulling things towards each other. Everything has a centre of gravity – big things and small. For example big planets are pulled into orbits by gravity and inside atoms there are miniature versions of the same thing happening. Even in my hand there are tiny things whirling about.

It would be really weird without gravity. Very funny things would happen. The rain might fly in all directions, maybe up instead of down. Sandy would float up towards the ceiling. Mum would have a tough job serving up SuperNoodles!

Some people say there are three dimensions, but there are more. When we are doing maths there are three – length, breadth and height. Time is another known dimension, the fourth. The fifth dimension is one no human can relate to. I know a bit about it

because of studying my cat, Sandy. The ultimate
dimension is Love and Truth. This dimension is the
same as eternity.

Understanding people with AS

AS people like me are minority people. This means I
am not like most other people and I might not make
the same choices or decisions. I like being a
minority person. I hate it when people don't accept
that I am a minority person. Like one time everyone
else wanted to go for a walk and I didn't. I felt really
hurt because they didn't understand about me being
a minority person. I ended up sitting on a rock on
my own till they came back.

Normal people should try harder to understand
AS people because AS people have difficulties with
some things most people find easy. They have to
work very hard to understand normal people and
behave normally. I know this because of how hard I
have had to work on things. Like my behaviour for
example. Before I started all the work I used to have
temper tantrums. This happened if I didn't get
exactly what I wanted, for example toys or attention
– anything at all really. I felt pretty miserable a lot of
the time and I hated not getting everything my own
way. Nowadays I am getting much more mature, but

it takes a lot of work. Sometimes I get fed up with it all and then I stay in my room for ages.

People should understand that it can be tough having AS. Small things can still really upset me sometimes. Like the other day when I couldn't find my sunglasses. This led to a lot of trouble for everyone because of me going berserk. It got so bad in the end that I felt like jumping out in front of the next car. I just didn't care. And then afterwards I felt really sad when I thought about how I had behaved.

Or when I lose a game – I just *hate* that. The way I might feel then is so bad I can't find words to explain it. Rage isn't a strong enough word. But I try very hard to remember to be a good sport. I am doing much better on this now.

Sometimes I forget all the things I have learned and go back to my old ways. Like last week when I wanted one of my ABA prizes right away without earning the tokens. It was all my fault that the ABA got cancelled. I was so angry with myself afterwards. This always happens. When I am upset I never take responsibility. I blame everybody else. Then when I calm down and relax I can see what has gone wrong.

Sometimes, when I get in a bad mood, Mum uses the timer to give me time to settle down and think. The timer is very helpful. I have to decide if I am going to change my behaviour before the timer beeps. Timers are very helpful. I use them a lot. For eating for example. Or getting my jammies on. She also uses ABA for this type of problem and they are happening far less now.

Also, sometimes I can get a lot of depression. These times make me feel that life is a downward spiral. Every bit of my body feels grey shafts of lightning pain and I feel like banging my head on the wall or something.

These are difficult problems to have. But I think the reason God gives people difficulties is to give them a chance to become stronger. I have my heart set on finding God's will and this doesn't ever change. Once you've decided to start the search for wisdom, you can't stop.

Helping AS kids

Kids who are different should not have to do things which are pointless just to be the same as other kids. For example some kids with autism don't like to speak. That is because they don't see the point in it. That's just the way I feel about handwriting. So they shouldn't be forced to speak if they don't want to.

It's silly to try and make people do things which are pointless to them. I hate doing things which are pointless. Anyway wisdom and kindness are more important than a lot of the things you learn at school.

Why do adults try to make children do things which are pointless? One of those things is handwriting. I hate writing things – even vertical or horizontal adding. Arithmetic is not my strong point anyway. I like using a calculator best, and I prefer the more interesting maths.

On this planet adults always think they know best but there is absolutely no justification for that. Some adults are OK though. I wouldn't like to go and live on another planet because I would miss my family.

Kids with autism need to get a lot of support. At school sometimes other children said things to me which were too mean to repeat. Some other kids were kind. Like one girl called Amy. She gave me a book to keep, because she knew how much I loved books. Other kids need to understand about people who are different. It would be a very boring world if everyone was the same, wouldn't it? Everyone would make the same decisions and do the same things and it would be so boring.

It is not at all fair to punish kids with autism. Instead of punishing them, parents should try using ABA. I use it a lot. It is really good fun. Before I knew about ABA I was always getting into trouble and this only made me worse. Now my behaviour is getting better and better all the time. Adults can be very unfair to children. Because of ABA this doesn't happen so much for me any more. ABA is far better than punishment.

I would definitely recommend any AS kid to try ABA. In fact any kid at all.

The *Titanic*

The *Titanic* was a famous ship which sank killing thousands of people when it hit an iceberg. It was a great disaster. The worst of it was it did not need to happen. The humans made a big mistake to say it was unsinkable. They said it was the fastest ship. But it never got there.

Imagine going through the sea at top speed when there were lots of icebergs in the water. This was just done to show off.

I think the sinking of the *Titanic* was a very sad disaster because so many people died, and what do humans do? Make a film about it. I think it is wrong to use it for entertainment. The next thing they will be making a film about the Omagh bombing. I would never go to see a film like this.

Rules

If I were King I would make fair laws and everyone would be equal. But there is always someone breaking laws. It doesn't matter what you say, people always disobey rules. For example it is illegal to kill elephants and take their ivory, but people still do it. People are always ignoring rules. That's just the way it is.

In Heaven everything is perfect. We must have patience to find our perfectness. This will happen when God decides. Things on this earth aren't perfect, but this is for our own good. Otherwise God would have made it perfect like Heaven.

AS and autism

Children with AS are the best experts about AS. They can tell adults what seems unusual to them about the world. If they tell this to the adults, the adults should do all in their power to make things right for the child. They should try to make their child feel at home. I never used to feel at home at all. In the last house where I lived I didn't feel so much at home as I do now. It used to be a lot worse. In the house I live in now I feel more at home because this is where we found out about my AS. That makes it feel more homely to me.

Some AS kids have special gifts. I read that some AS kids can count thousands of matches if they are dropped on the floor. They know the exact number just by looking at them. I think this is really cool. I have also got a gift in maths but I can't count matches like that. It would be cool to be able to do that. Those kids must be very smart. My Mum did not know I had a gift with maths until Jacinta told her. When I was at school I didn't do much maths at all and I hated writing down every kind of sum. Some AS kids find school very boring because of the way things are taught.

For me, AS and autism are the same thing. It is very hard to tell what AS is. It is very hard to describe and nobody really knows for sure. Not even the experts or the people who have it. I don't even know what AS is for sure but I think it is a kind of gift. I don't know what is would be like to be normal. It is very hard for me to imagine that.

I don't think of it as a disability. Some people have physical disabilities where they have to be in a wheelchair. It is not painful unless it is very severe.

I don't normally tell people I have AS but it is not a disability for me. One thing I hate is when people use the word 'suffer', and say I 'suffer' from autism. It is not something I suffer from, it's just the way I am. I don't tell them they suffer from being normal, do I?

I like most things about AS but one thing I don't like is not being able to eat normally. Sometimes I pray that the next day I will be able to eat like other kids. I do my best, but eating is something which is very hard for me. It's not that I can't do it but something stops me from doing it. I don't know what that thing is. This eating problem is really the only bad thing about AS for me.

Sometimes people say they want to build a bridge between normal people and autism. I feel like a new country in the world that no-one can discover, and I don't want a bridge built right across to me. I am not at all happy that this bridge has been started and it must never be allowed to be complete. Otherwise normal people might try to become autistic and autistic people might try to become normal. In the end they might succeed, and there will be no more autistic people. This would be against God's laws for sure.

My future

I prefer not to worry about the future. I haven't decided what I will become when I grow up but I hope to be happy and healthy. I would like to do something to make the world a better place.

Useful Addresses

National Association for Gifted Children
540 Elder House
Milton Keynes
MK9 1LR
Tel: 01908 673677

For further information about Asperger Syndrome, you can contact:

The National Autistic Society
393 City Road
London EC1V 1NE
Tel: 020 7833 2299

Autism Society of America Inc.
7910 Woodmont Avenue, Suite 650
Bethesda
MD 20814–3015
USA
Tel: 301 657 0881

Autism Society of Canada
129 Yorkville Avenue, Suite 202
Toronto
Ontario M5R 1C4
Canada
Tel: 416 922 0302

The ASPEN (Asperger Syndrome Education Network) Society of America Inc.
PO Box 2577
Jacksonville
FL 32203–2577
USA
Tel: 904 745 6741

Asperger's Syndrome Support Network
c/o VACCA
PO Box 235
Ashburton
Victoria 3147
Australia

Autistic Association of New Zealand
PO Box 7305
Sydenham
Christchurch
New Zealand
Tel: 03 332 1038

Parents and Professionals and Autism (The Northern Ireland Autism Charity)
Knockbracken Healthcare Park
Saintfield Road
Belfast BT8 8BH
Tel: 028 90 401 729

Parents Education as Autism Therapists
1 Acrebank
Whitehead
Carrick Fergus BT38 9TD
Tel: 028 9337 8769

Websites

National Autistic Society
www.oneworld.org/autism_uk/index.html

OASIS (Online Asperger Syndrome Information and Support)
www.udel.edu/bkirby/asperger/

The Centre for the Study of Autism
www.autism.org

Asperger's Disorder Homepage
www.aspergers.com